BEAUTIFUL
SOUTH AFRICA

CLB 1976
This edition published 1990 by Central News Agency Ltd,
Laub Street, New Centre, Johannesburg, South Africa.
© 1987 Colour Library Books Ltd, Godalming, Surrey, England.
Printed and bound by Leefung Asco Printers Ltd, Hong Kong.
All rights reserved.
ISBN 0 86283 561 5

BEAUTIFUL
SOUTH AFRICA

CNa

After the *Haerlem* ran aground in Table Bay on March 25th 1647, the crew's positive reports of the hospitable land they found there paved the way for permanent European settlement in 1652. From the beginnings of their new city of Cape Town, early European settlers discovered the wider outlines and natural riches of the new land. From Cape Town the great plains of the central plateau spread north and east, forming a massive basin which comprises most of the country. In their journeyings, pioneers would have come upon only small and shallow rivers, many leading into the central drainage system of the Orange River, and at the western and far eastern edges of the plains they would have met with the mountains of the Great Escarpment, dividing the plateau from the narrow coastal plain.

In places the plateau they explored is dramatically flat, in others rolling, and is spread with wide areas of veld grassland, parklike savanna or bushveld and the dry, sandy dunes and scrubland of the Kalahari. The sedimentary rocks of the Transvaal and Free State High Veld, for example, have been eroded to form an essentially flat landscape, broken only by gorge-like river channels, residual mountains and prominent, isolated hills or kopjes. Large areas of the highveld are covered with salt pans, and across it spreads grassveld vegetation, dominated by species of tall red grass. The open, level character of this highveld and the availability of water in the valleys was particularly welcoming to the early settlers. Consequently, they and those who followed chose this place to establish many farms and towns. The highveld is now extensively cultivated – most of South Africa's maize crop is grown across the former grassveld – and selectively grazed, and the region's mineral resources have encouraged the growth of industry. Being the most hospitable, the highveld has become the most populated area of South Africa, and much of its animal life has, therefore, disappeared.

In marked contrast were the unwelcoming expanses of the Kalahari Desert in the west. Here there is little permanent surface water, and the plateau spreads in gentle, sand-covered undulations, its sameness disrupted only by the occasional range of hills formed of older, harder rock. However, despite the sand and the erratic supplies of water, the Kalahari has a rich and complex vegetation cover, well-adapted to the dry conditions. In the South African section of the desert, thorny woodland is interspersed with parkland and low to the ground grow various grasses and shrubs, water-storing tuberous and bulbous plants, creepers and vines. Because of the area's relative inhospitality to man, and the protection of the Kalahari Gemsbok National Park, much of its wildlife remains intact. Even in this drier southern section,

the Kalahari's rich rollcall of animal life includes the magnificent gemsbok, hartebeest, springbok, wildebeest, eland and the diminutive duiker.

Above these plains landscapes rises South Africa's most sustained mountain feature, the Great Escarpment, a dramatic barrier to the early pioneers. Known by a series of local names as it marches around the basin, the range begins as the Transvaal Drakensberg in the northeast, reaches its highest points, up to 11,000 feet, further south in the Natal Drakensberg, and extends into southern Cape Province. The eastern side of the range is deeply cut in many places by green river valleys, while the western edge shelves away gently to the flatness of the central plateau. Topped with snow in winter, much of the range remains wild and unspoilt in its remoteness, and much appreciated by visitors to its resorts and camping grounds. Well-supplied with water, some of the lower slopes of the escarpment support great plantations, amongst which survive patches of the indigenous forest of red stinkwoods, ironwoods, yellow-woods, cabbage trees and the beautiful rooi hout. Higher up grow cypresses, sagewood trees, mountain cycad, evergreen sugar bush and colourful protea.

Beyond the great barrier of the Transvaal Drakensberg to the northeast, pioneers came upon an area of parklike lowveld, where the plains are broken by low ridges or groups of island mountains and the soils are comparatively fertile and water-retaining. These conditions support not just grassland but a rich variety of plant cover. In higher areas typical trees are acacia and maroola and the ground-cover mostly red-grass, while at lower altitudes, such as along the valleys of the Sabi and Letaba rivers, the red grass is replaced by tufted finger grasses, euphorbias and other succulents, the trees include larger acacias, mopane trees, wild fig, ancient, bulbous boababs and the tall fan palm tree, and the banks of the rivers are lined with lush gallery forest. In this region lie the 19,010 square kilometres of Kruger National Park, where the lowveld habitats are protected and preserved in the undisturbed state necessary for their native inhabitants to prosper. Herds of Burchell's zebra, blue wildebeest and antelopes from the large eland to the graceful impala spread across the grassland, grazing on sweetgrass and tamboekie or browsing amongst acacia thornbushes and red bush-willow. Upon these prey lions, leopards and cheetahs, hippopotamuses and crocodiles wallow in the Great Letaba, elephants and rhinoceroses move ponderously through the bush and giraffes feed on the topmost branches of acacia trees, presenting a precious, living picture of the incredible wealth of African landscape and wildlife which thrived all across this country when its vastness was first explored by Europeans.

Facing page: tower blocks in central Cape Town.

Right and overleaf left: the setting sun silhouettes Table Mountain and Lion's Head, and (facing page) Lion's Head towers over Cape Town and the surf-fringed coastline. Below: the Atlantic shoreline of the Peninsula, dominated by the massive bulk of the Twelve Apostles. Overleaf right: the splendid, Greek-inspired Rhodes Memorial on the slopes of Devil's Peak in Groote Schuur estate, Cape Town.

Facing page: the rocky Atlantic shore of Clifton Bay backed by the peaks of the Twelve Apostles, and (top) a leisurely game of bowls. Cape Town's old City Hall (right), built in 1893, forms a focal point for the area known as the Grand Parade, with its daily fruit and flower market (above) and its flea market (right). Overleaf: the modern face of Cape Town.

Facing page: (bottom) the colourful homeliness of Kalk Bay's beach huts, and (top) the all-weather observation post at the Cape of Good Hope. Above: one of the four sheltered beaches of Clifton Bay. Overleaf: (left) a car park above the rocks at Sea Point, and (right) the seawater swimming pool on Sea Point Promenade, backed by the luxury hotels and apartments lining Beach Road, Cape Town.

There are over 22,000 species of wildflower in South Africa, and the Western Cape is said to contain the richest concentration of flowering plants in the world. This page: some of the many beautiful varieties in the Cape of Good Hope Nature Reserve, a vast, natural flower garden at the foot of the Cape Peninsula, and at Kirstenbosch, on the slopes of Table Mountain, devoted exclusively to the cultivation of indigenous plants. Among these are (top centre) helichrysum or everlasting flowers, (above far left) the pincushion and (above) the King Protea, South Africa's floral emblem. Facing page: a gregarious, and seemingly-contented colony of jackass penguins on Marcus Island, at the entrance to Saldanha Bay, about sixty miles north of Cape Town. The jackass penguin flourishes along the west coast of Africa from the Cape to Angola. Overleaf: (left) the University of Cape Town, and (right) Cape Point and its precariously-perched lighthouse.

Boschendal estate (facing page), one of the Rhodes Fruit Farms, was bought by Cecil Rhodes in 1896. The 19th-century building housing the Theological Seminary of Stellenbosch (above) stands in the town of that name (previous pages), the Cape's second oldest settlement. Top: Doornbosch, at Stellenbosch, a restaurant run by the Wine Farmers' Co-operative of this wine-producing area (right).

Previous pages: (left) the University of Stellenbosch and (right) the world-famous Blue Train speeding through the Hex River Valley. Left: the Afrikaans Language Monument at Paarl and (above) the memorial to the Huguenots who settled at Franschhoek in the 1680s and contributed greatly to the development of the Cape wine industry (remaining pictures).

Above: the lovely countryside around Caledon in the southern Cape and (facing page) the Lanzerac winery. The Breë River Valley is the largest of the wine and fruit producing regions of the western Cape, and Worcester (overleaf left) is its main town, a bustling commercial and industrial centre. Overleaf right: a patchwork landscape near Wellington.

Ladismith (facing page), situated at the western end of the Swartberg Mountains in the Little Karoo, is noted for ostrich farming. The heartland of South Africa is a the huge, hot, dry area of the Great Karoo. The invigorating and health-giving air of this region led to the development of Matjiesfontein (above), a once-fashionable Victorian health and holiday resort.

From Cape Agulhas (facing page bottom and above) to Storms River lie seascapes (remaining pictures) of great natural beauty, reflecting the Indian Ocean in all its moods. Nowhere is the scene more beautiful than at Knysna Heads (facing page top), protecting a great lagoon, or at nearby Buffelsbaai (top).

Beacon Island (above) derives its name from the beacon that Governor Plettenberg erected to claim Beacon Bay for the Dutch East India Company. Since then the island has been the site of a Norwegian whaling station and is now a popular holiday resort, its modern hotel overlooking jagged, seaworn rocks. Facing page: the beach at Walker Point. Overleaf: (left) rocky coast near Knysna and (right) the lighthouse at Cape St. Francis.

Above: the fragmented coastline of the Tsitsikama Forest and Coastal national parks. The Paul Sauer Bridge (facing page), spanning the spectacular gorge of the Storms River, was officially opened in 1964. Designed by Ricardo Morandi of Rome, it was built on the principle of a castle drawbridge, two sections being hinged onto platforms on either side of the river and lowered to meet in the centre.

The reddish Addo elephant (left) lives in Addo Elephant National Park. Smaller than the African elephant and with rounder ears, they were hunted almost to extinction early this century. Protected by the park, the herd now numbers about 130. Top left and top centre: ostriches, farmed at Oudtshoorn. Above: a steamtrain, and (right) the beach, at Wilderness. Top: one of the Knysna Heads.

Left: the City Hall of Port Elizabeth, Cape Province, and (top) red cliffs beside Bavianskloof, a 95-mile-long scenic road west of the city. Above: the Cape-Dutch Reinet House Museum, (facing page top) the town hall, and (facing page bottom) a fine Dutch Reformed church at the end of Church Street, in Graaff-Reinet in the Karoo.

Facing page: a sandy bay on the Wild Coast of the Transkei. South of Durban, the coast of Natal is blessed with a high rainfall, rich soil and temperatures ranging from warm to hot and humid, which make it a green, lush area and a popular holiday resort. Above: luxury homes near Palm Beach in Natal.

Right and top: modern hotels in the resort of Umhlanga Rocks on the north coast of Natal. Ideally located on the shores of the great natural harbour of Port Natal, Durban (top right and above) is the main port of South Africa, handling a large proportion of its sea trade. Durban also thrives on its attraction as an exciting luxury holiday resort.

51

Shore fishing in Durban Harbour and along the beaches (left) can be very rewarding. Barracuda, greenfish, kingfish, shad and garrick may be caught between July and November - early in the morning and just before sunset. Above: the Victoria Embankment overlooking the harbour, and (facing page) relaxing on the beach, at Durban. Backing the beach is the Marine Parade, lined on the west side with modern hotels and on the east with a three-kilometre-long strip of holiday entertainments, including amusement parks, an aquarium, a snake park and bowling greens. Overleaf: the City Hall and War Memorial, Durban.

Previous pages: Marine Parade and the aquarium and amusement parks along Durban's beachfront, and (facing page) the white hotels of Umhlanga Rocks. Above: the coastline north of Durban, where the noise and crowds of the city give way to peaceful green hills and secluded bays.

Above: St Lucia Estuary, part of the game reserve of Lake St Lucia in Kwazulu, and (facing page) the Kosi Bay area on the coast of Tongaland, at the mouth of a chain of lakes. Situated on the edge of the highveld, Piet Retief (overleaf left) is named after the Voortrekker leader murdered by the Zulus in 1838 and is a center for the paper-making industry. Overleaf right: the fertile valley of Ohrigstad, resettled in the 1920s after its first European population was wiped out by malaria in the late 19th century.

The incredible variety of South Africa's wildlife (these pages), gone from the vast areas now occupied by farms, towns and industry, is preserved in protected parks. Facing page: (top left) gemsbok, (bottom left) the Kalahari lion, distinguished from other African lions by its tawny mane, (above) springbok, and (left) rhinoceros on the Sabi Sabi game ranch in the Eastern Transvaal.

These pages: the luxury international tourist resort of Sun City, set in the dramatic scenery of the Pilanesberg Range of Bophuthatswana. The Pilanesberg consists of six concentric mountain rings formed by volcanic action and enclosing at their centre a rich game reserve. Overleaf: farming across the golden plains of the western Transvaal.

Above: the green of farm gardens in the western Transvaal, and (facing page) the elaborate modern design of the Bophuthatswana Government Offices in Mmabatho. The memorial (overleaf) to 2,683 South African soldiers who died at Delville Wood in France during the First World War stands in the terraced gardens of Sir Herbert Baker's Union Buildings on Meintjeskop, overlooking Pretoria.

Sir Herbert Baker's Union Buildings (above and top), surrounded by magnificent terraced gardens (right), dominate South Africa's capital city of Pretoria from the top of Meintjeskop. The Voortrekker Monument (left), in southern Pretoria, commemorates the indomitable spirit of the 19th-century Afrikaner pioneers of the Great Trek.

The site of Pretoria (these pages) was first settled by migrating Nguni-speaking people, now known as the Matabele, about 350 years ago. Similarly attracted by the two sheltered, warm and fertile valleys on which Pretoria now stands, the Voortrekkers established several farms along the valley of the Apies in 1837, and in 1853 the valley was chosen as the site for the capital of the South African Republic. Facing page: the orderly city seen from the Observation Deck of the Volkskas Centre and (above and right) the red-roofed Union Buildings.

Near the neoclassical Union Buildings in Pretoria are a number of elegant ministerial houses (facing page). The Loftus Versfeld Rugby Stadium (above), to the south of Church Street in Pretoria, seats 66,000. Overleaf: (left) the University of Pretoria, the republic's largest full-time university, and also an important cultural centre, housing the Aula theatre complex. (Right) the Union Buildings on Meintjeskop, Pretoria, fronted by formal gardens.

The massive Voortrekker Monument, designed by Gerhard Moerdyk, was erected to commemorate the Great Trek, undertaken between 1835 and 1854 by about 6,000 Afrikaner farmers who left Cape Colony and journeyed north to establish themselves in what became the Orange Free State, Natal and the Transvaal. Facing page: the green residential areas and distant towers of Pretoria. Overleaf: the highveld city of Johannesburg by night.

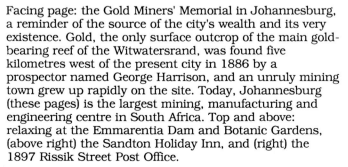

Facing page: the Gold Miners' Memorial in Johannesburg, a reminder of the source of the city's wealth and its very existence. Gold, the only surface outcrop of the main gold-bearing reef of the Witwatersrand, was found five kilometres west of the present city in 1886 by a prospector named George Harrison, and an unruly mining town grew up rapidly on the site. Today, Johannesburg (these pages) is the largest mining, manufacturing and engineering centre in South Africa. Top and above: relaxing at the Emmarentia Dam and Botanic Gardens, (above right) the Sandton Holiday Inn, and (right) the 1897 Rissik Street Post Office.

Facing page: the Wanderers' Golf Club and the Wanderers' Club playing fields and cricket stadium, Johannesburg. Above: the slender JG Strijdom Post Office Tower above Johannesburg's high-rise blocks and its streets clouded with purple jacaranda trees. Overleaf: (left) central Johannesburg, its suburbs stretching far into the distance, and (right) the city's Ellis Park Stadium, which seats over 70,000 spectators and is the home of the Transvaal Rugby Union.

The peaceful town of Clarens (facing page), in the eastern Free State, was named in memory of Paul Kruger, who died in exile in Clarens, Switzerland in 1904. Nearby is the Golden Gate Highlands National Park (above), where coloured sandstone has been eroded into striking formations. Overleaf: the Royal Natal National Park (left), at the northern end of Natal's Drakensberg Range, lies at the foot of the beautiful Mont-aux-Sources. (Right) the Caledon River gorge.

SECTION LOOKING EAST	The Kimberley Mine	
	DISCOVERED 16TH JULY 1871 BY FLEETWOOD RAWSTONE	
	AREA AT SURFACE	17 ha
	PERIMETER	1.6 km
	AXIS NORTH & SOUTH	500 m
	AXIS EAST & WEST	457 m
	SURFACE TO TOP OF HARD ROCK	90 m
	SURFACE TO WATER	165 m
	DEPTH OF WATER	230 m
	GROUND EXCAVATED	22.500.000 t
	DIAMONDS PRODUCED	14.504.566 carats
	EQUIVALENT TO	2722 kg
	WORKING CEASED	AUGUST 1914

The Kimberley Mine (top and overleaf) and
its vital statistics (above) tell part of the story
of this city built on diamond profits.
Kimberley was founded with the New Rush of
1871, following the 'dry ground' discovery of
diamonds on the De Beer family farm in May.
Among the prospectors was a group led by
Fleetwood Rawstone from Colesberg, and it
was they who made the first discovery on the
Colesberg Koppie, now the Big Hole of
Kimberley Mine. Right: an open-air museum
reviving early mining scenes, and (facing
page) diamond diggers honoured in bronze.

Above: farmland near Warrenton, which developed as a major vegetable producer to meet the demand from Kimberley, and (facing page) Jan Kempdorp, the dry land around it made fertile by Cecil Rhodes' scheme to irrigate the valleys of the Vaal and Harts rivers, Cape Province. Overleaf: (left) the Sishen Iron Ore Mine, southwest of Kuruman in Cape Province, where workings colour the land from mauves to the red of iron ore deposits. (Right) land around Kuruman.

Facing page: the endless, arid terrain of northern Cape Province. The landscape of the vast Kalahari Gemsbok National Park (above and overleaf) is similarly semi-desert, consisting of red sand dunes, scattered vegetation and bush-covered watercourses. Amongst these thrive thousands of springbok, together with gemsbok, red hartebeest, eland, kudu, hyena, cheetah and tawny-maned lion.

Above: the green band of well-watered, cultivated land along the Orange River Valley near Upington. The thunder of nearby Augrabies Falls (facing page) reaches its height in a peak flood, when over 400 million litres of water from the Orange River plunge into the 240-metre-deep gorge every minute. Overleaf: (left) the Bokkeveld plateau, (right) Cape Columbine in Swartland. Following page: Green Point and Sea Point, Cape Town.